*Really Wild*

# PUMAS

**Stephanie St. Pierre**

Heinemann LIBRARY

**www.heinemann.co.uk**
Visit our website to find out more information about Heinemann Library books.

To order:
 Phone 44 (0) 1865 888066
 Send a fax to 44 (0) 1865 314091
 Visit the Heinemann Bookshop at www.heinemann.co.uk to browse our catalogue and order online.

First published in Great Britain by Heinemann Library,
Halley Court, Jordan Hill, Oxford OX2 8EJ,
a division of Reed Educational and Professional Publishing Ltd.
Heinemann is a registered trademark of Reed Educational and
Professional Publishing Ltd.

OXFORD  MELBOURNE  AUCKLAND
JOHANNESBURG  BLANTYRE  GABORONE
IBADAN  PORTSMOUTH (NH)  USA  CHICAGO

© Reed Educational and Professional Publishing Ltd 2002
The moral right of the proprietor has been asserted.

Designed by Depke Design
Originated by Ambassador Litho Ltd
Printed and bound by South China Printing in Hong
Kong/China

ISBN 0 431 02905 9 (hardback)
06 05 04 03 02
10 9 8 7 6 5 4 3 2 1

ISBN 0 431 02910 5 (paperback)
06 05 04 03 02
10 9 8 7 6 5 4 3 2 1

British Library Cataloguing in Publication Data

St. Pierre, Stephanie
Pumas – (Really wild) (Take-off!)
1. Pumas – Juvenile literature
I. Title
599.7'524

Acknowledgements
The publishers would like to thank the following for permission to
reproduce photographs: Nick Wheeler/Corbis, p. 4 (far left); Tom
Brakefield/Corbis, pp. 4 (centre), 14; Lynda Richardson/Corbis,
p. 4 (far right); Dr. Robert Franz/Corbis, pp. 5, 18, 22; Stuart
Westmorland/Corbis, p. 6; W. Perry Conway/Corbis, pp. 7, 8, 12;
Leonard Lee Rue III/Photo Researchers Inc., p. 9; Amy & Chuck
Wiley/Wales/Index Stock Imagery/PictureQuest, p. 10; Mary
Ann McDonald/Corbis, p. 11; Joe McDonald/Corbis, pp. 13, 15;
Larry Lipsky/Index Stock, p. 19; William Dow/Corbis, pp. 16,
17; David A. Northcott/Corbis, p. 20; Steve Kaufman/Corbis, p.
21; Edward K. Degginger/Bruce Colman, p.23.

Cover photograph reproduced with permission of NHPA/Andy
Rouse.

Our thanks to Sue Graves and Hilda Reed for their advice and
expertise in the preparation of this book.

Disclaimer
All the Internet addresses (URLs) given in this book were valid at
the time of going to press. However, due to the dynamic nature of
the Internet, some addresses may have changed, or sites may have
ceased to exist since publication. While the author and publishers
regret any inconvenience this may cause readers, no responsibility
for any such changes can be accepted by either the author or the
publishers.

# Contents

Any words appearing in the text in bold, **like this**, are explained in the glossary.

# The puma and its relatives

Pumas are **felines**. All cats, including house cats, jaguars and lions are felines. The jaguar is the only cat in North and South America bigger than the puma.

puma

house cat

jaguar

All these cats are felines.

Pumas have light tan or brown fur.

All pumas are close relatives. They have small round ears and long thick tails. Their fur is brown or light tan. The puma has white fur on its belly.

# Where pumas live

Pumas once lived all over North and South America. A few pumas still live in Florida, but most pumas in the United States live in the western part of the country now.

North America

Florida

South America

N
W E
S

puma

The red parts of the map show where pumas are found.

A male puma will chase away other males that come into its home range.

A puma likes to find a good look-out spot.

Each puma lives in its own **home range**. A puma needs fresh water, **prey** and places to rest. Female pumas also need **dens** for hiding their **kittens**.

# The family

Pumas are very shy and quiet. They live alone and stay away from each other except when they **mate**.

puma                                        undergrowth

Pumas like to hide in undergrowth like this.

This puma puts its scent on sticks to mark its boundary.

The first male puma to arrive in an area marks its **home range** with its scent and scratches together piles of sticks and dirt at its **boundaries**. This tells other pumas to stay away.

# Jumping

Pumas are the best jumpers of all cats. A puma can jump straight up the side of a rock cliff.

A puma can sometimes jump as high as a two-storey house!

This puma can easily leap from one rock to another.

A puma has powerful legs to help it jump.

A puma can jump a long distance straight ahead when running. It can jump as long as half a tennis court!

# Hunting

Pumas hunt large animals, like elk and deer. They will hunt day or night depending on the **prey** they are after.

puma

prey

Pumas use their flexible backs and tails to turn at speed and catch their prey.

Pumas, like all cats, use their keen hearing to help search for prey.

The puma spends a lot of time looking for prey. The puma's strength, speed and jumping help it to make a **kill**.

# Eating

The puma may hide its **kill** in a **cache**, burying it under leaves and sticks. The puma will come back to eat from the cache for several days.

Sometimes coyotes or wolves will find a puma's cache and eat all the food.

puma

kill

coyote

This coyote wants to steal the puma's kill.

snowshoe hare

This puma has caught a snowshoe hare.

If they can find no large **prey**, pumas will
eat animals such as porcupines, racoons, birds
and even mice.

# Babies

There are usually two or three **kittens** in a puma **litter**. Kittens are playful. When they are about two months old the kittens leave the secret **den** where they were born.

kittens

puma mother

Puma kittens keep safe in their den.

Pumas **mate** so that their kittens are born in the spring. This means the kittens will be almost grown before the next winter sets in.

Kittens learn a lot from following their mother.

From the time they leave the den the kittens will follow their mother when she hunts. Kittens stay with their mothers for up to two years.

# Growing up

Once puma **kittens** have learned to hunt they must find their own place to live. Grown pumas will fight young pumas that enter their **home range**.

grown puma

Cats like the puma do not like others near them because they compete for **prey**.

young puma

A grown puma attacks a young one.

One of the most dangerous times for a young puma is when it first leaves its mother to find a place to live.

Pumas may fight to the death to protect their home ranges.

Young pumas may be killed before they get a chance to find a place of their own.

# Danger

People are the puma's worst enemy. Pumas usually stay away from people. But when people build houses in a puma's **home range**, the puma may try to chase them away.

house

puma

Some people build their homes where pumas live.

Pumas are also called cougars, mountain lions or panthers.

PANTHER CROSSING NEXT 7 MI.

Signs like these warn people that pumas live in the area.

Many pumas are killed because they come too close to people. Pumas rarely attack humans or **livestock**, but many people still fear these cats.

# Puma facts

A puma:

- purrs but does not meow
- makes a sound like a growl and a yowl together
- will flatten its ears when angry.

An angry puma will growl and flatten its ears.

A puma will climb a tree if it is in danger.

A puma:
- can climb trees to escape its enemies
- will climb trees or rocks to look over its home range
- can grow to about two metres long.

# Glossary

**boundaries** imaginary lines that separate places

**cache** hiding place for food

**den** place where wild animals live or hide

**feline** member of the family of animals that includes all kinds of cats

**habitat** home or place where something lives

**home range** area of land that a big cat lives on

**kill** dead animal that has been caught for food

**kitten** puma baby

**livestock** animals that people keep for food

**mate** when a male and female animal come together to make babies

**predator** animal that hunts other animals for food

**prey** animals that are hunted and killed by other animals

**yowl** loud, strange crying sound

# Index

# More books to read

*Big Cats* by Sarah Walker (Eye Wonder series), Dorling Kindersley, 2002

*Big Cats* by Sandra Woodcock (Livewire Investigates series), Hodder and Stoughton Educational, 2001